SERMON OUTLINES

Prophetic Themes

T0312557

compiled by
Al Bryant

kregel
PUBLICATIONS

Grand Rapids, MI 49501

Sermon Outlines on Prophetic Themes by Al Bryant

Copyright © 1993 by Kregel Publications, a division of Kregel, Inc., P.O. Box 2607, Grand Rapids, MI 49501. Kregel Publications provides trusted, biblical publications for Christian growth and service. Your comments and suggestions are valued.

Library of Congress Cataloging-in-Publication Data
Bryant, Al (1926–
    Sermon outlines on prophetic themes / [compiled by] Al Bryant.
        p.   cm.
Includes index.
    1. Bible—Prophecies—Sermons—Outlines, syllabi, etc. I. Bryant, Al, 1926–
BS647.2.S47   1993   251'.02—dc20   92-23982
                                                                        CIP
ISBN 0-8254-2087-3

2 3 4 5 6 / 07 06 05 04 03

Printed in the United States of America

SERMON OUTLINES

on

Prophetic Themes

Also by Al Bryant

CONTENTS

PREFACE

Christians believe that God has a program for His world, and for the people He has placed in it. He reveals this program in His Word. Since prophecy is such a crucial link in the understanding of that plan of God, it is vital that messages on prophetic themes, especially the Second Coming of Jesus Christ, be regularly presented in the church, so that believers, and unbelievers too, will be often reminded that this earthly life is not "all there is."

The outlines chosen for this compilation have been selected because of their very real and effective approach to Bible prophecy. Undogmatic and Bible-centered, they are slanted toward believers, but with application to unbelievers as well. It is the hope of both compiler and publisher that the use of these messages will be an effective means of challenging Christians to a closer walk and a greater understanding of God's will for their lives, and a means of reaching into the very hearts of unbelievers, shaking them loose from their preconceived notions about "religion" and its place in one's life. May these outlines help you, and may they be a source of blessing and challenge to those to whom you speak.

In using these outlines, you may want to remove the sheet (or sheets) from the book and place them in your Bible or ring binder.

Al Bryant

THE THREE ADVENTS:
A KEY TO SACRED HISTORY

Acts 1:1-11

I.   **Creation the Main Advent**
    A.   Creation of the world (Gen. 1:1).
    B.   Creation of man (Gen. 1:26).
    C.   The fall of man (Gen. 3:1-7).
    D.   The curse upon the race (Gen. 3:18).
    E.   Promise of a redeemer—The Christ (Gen. 3:15).

II.   **The First Advent of Christ**
    A.   Incarnation (John 1:14; Matt. 1:18-21).
    B.   Manifestation (John 1:33,34; Matt. 3:16).
    C.   Crucifixion—Christ dying (Matt. 27:35-39).
    D.   Resurrection (John 20:17; Acts 1:3).
    E.   Ascension (Acts 1:19).
    F.   The descent and gift of the Holy Spirit (Acts 2:1-4).

III.   **The Second Coming a Final Advent**
Six great consummations will then take place.
    A.   Redemption (Eph. 1:41).
    B.   Resurrection (John 5:29; 1 Cor. 15:40-44; Acts 24:15).
    C.   Restitution (Acts 3:19-21).
    D.   Regeneration (1 Cor. 4:17; Matt. 19:28).
    E.   Revelation (1 Peter 1:13; Jude 34).
    F.   Glorification (Matt. 23:39; 1 Thess. 4:15-18).

SELECTED

THREE APPEARINGS OF CHRIST

Hebrews 9:24-28

1.   He Once Appeared (v. 26)—Atonement.

2.   He Now Appears (v. 24)—Advocacy.

3.   He Shall Appear (v. 28)—Advent.

JOHN RITCHIE

THE BOOK OF THE REVELATION

1. It is a Book of stupendous facts.
Facts referring to the Church, the Jew, Israel, the Gentiles, Satan, the beast, the false prophet, heaven, hell, time, and eternity.

2. It is a Book of symbols.
Seals. Bowls. Trumpets.

3. It is a Book telling of present and future judgment.
Present judgment as brought out by Christ being in the midst of the churches, in the character in which He is seen; and the future in relation to the world, antichrist, Satan, Rome, and corrupt Christianity.

4. It is a Book full of precious realities.
See the "I knows" and the "I wills" of Christ to the seven churches. Also the "No mores."

5. It is a Book full of Old Testament allusions.
There are from 200 to 300 references and allusions to the Old Testament in this book. More than any one Gospel or Epistle.

6. It is a peculiar Book, if we contrast it with the Gospel and the Epistles of John.
In the Gospel of John, we have Christ as the One in whom we believe; in the Epistle, the One whom we love; and in the Revelation, as the One we are waiting for.

In the Gospel we see Christ as the Apostle, i.e., the sent One; in the Epistle, as our Advocate; and in the Revelation, as the King.

In the Gospel, it is His work on the Cross for us; in the Epistle, it is His work for us in heaven; in the Revelation, His work as Judge.

In the Gospel, we see Christ as the Word of God in creation and grace for us; in the Epistle, as the Word of Life manifested to us; and in the Revelation, as the Word of God in judgment.

7. It is a Book revealing Christ.
We see Christ as the great High Priest judging the evil in the churches; as the Lamb on the Throne; as the Object of worship in heaven; as the Man of war overthrowing His enemies; as the Judge judging the wicked; as the Bridegroom of His church; and as the King reigning in righteousness.

"Revelation of Jesus Christ"—not of John. Revelation—the unfolding or unveiling the Lord and His purpose. Where did Christ get the Revelation? "From His Father." What is its purpose? "To show unto His servants," etc. To whom are these things made known? "His servants," or, more correctly, His bond-slaves. It is the same word as in Revelation 6:15—"Bondman."

When are these things to take place? "Shortly," or speedily, same word as in Luke 18:8—"speedily."

F. E. MARSH

BUT WE SEE JESUS

1. Jesus who purged our sins (Heb. 1:3).

2. Jesus crowned with glory and honor (Heb. 2:9).

3. Jesus, the Author and Finisher of our faith (Heb. 12:2).

4. Jesus made a Surety (Heb. 7:22).

5. Jesus made a High Priest forever (Heb. 6:20).

6. A High Priest . . . holy, harmless, undefiled, separate from sinners (Heb. 7:26).

7. A merciful High Priest (Heb. 2:17).

8. A great High Priest (Heb. 4:14).

9. A High Priest who is set on the right hand of the Majesty in the heavens (Heb. 8:1); who is able to save to the uttermost, seeing He ever liveth (Heb. 7:25); And to them that look for Him, will He appear the second time without sin unto salvation (Heb. 9:28).

> Jesus is the name we treasure,
> Name beyond what words can tell;
> Name of gladness, name of pleasure,
> Ear and heart delighting well;
> Name of sweetness, passing measure.
> Saving us from sin and hell.

HANDFULS OF HELP

"THE GLORIES OF CHRIST" IN ZECHARIAH 6:11-13

I. He is the crowned High Priest (v. 11). The crowns are made of silver and gold. The one speaks of redemption—His death—and the other of His Divine glory as—the Son of God.

II. "The Man whose name is The Branch." This is Christ's special name in relation to Israel and their future glory (see Isa. 11:1; Jer. 23:5, and 33:15; Zech. 3:8); the Stone of Israel with seven eyes—the only times He is thus named.

III. His service for them and also for us. "He shall branch up under Him, and build the temple of the Lord; even He shall build the temple of the Lord." What He will yet do for Israel, and also His present work for His Father and for us, the Church of God (Eph. 2:19-22; 1 Cor. 3:9; Heb. 3:3; 1 Peter 2:4,5).

IV. He is the Glory-Bearer. "And He shall bear the glory." It is only by Him, and in Him, and from Him, that all God's eternal blessings of His salvation come to us, and soon will to Israel. How glorious He is! "On His head are many crowns."

V. He will be the reigning and ruling One. "He shall sit and rule on His throne." We see Him now as our enthroned Sin-Purger, Prophet, Priest, and Lord, and soon He will be known and loved as Israel's Redeemer and King. His Kingly reign and glory, and all its Divine issues, will then be fulfilled, known, and delighted in by them.

VI. "The counsel of peace between them both," which speaks of the infinite delight He will have in all those He has so divinely blessed, and also of their delight and peace they will have in Him. Blessed be God for the prospect!

W. H.

HOPE THE ANCHOR OF THE SOUL

"Which hope we have as an anchor of the soul, both sure and stead-fast, and which entereth into that within the veil" (Heb. 6:19).

Let us consider, from this passage, the Nature, Characteristics, Importance, and Certainty of the Christian's Hope.

I. The Nature of Christian Hope.

Hope is the earnest desire of some future good.

A. The object is always really or imaginarily good. What is evil is an object of fear, dislike, and dread. Object of the Christian's hope is the enjoyment of God, the true good. The enjoyment of His favor, smiles, and blessings to the end of life. And the enjoyment of His presence forevermore.

B. The object of hope must be future good. Hope can never be exercised in reference to the past; and what we now possess, why should we hope for it? It is its peculiar province to be expecting, to be looking forward. Christian hope looks forward for the enjoyment of what God has laid up for them who love Him.

C. The object of hope must be attainable. It may be connected with difficulties, but there must still be a possibility of possessing it. The Christian's hope is built on a foundation that can never fail; "For God will withhold no good thing from them that walk uprightly." Notice,

II. The Characteristics of This Hope.

"Which hope we have as an anchor of the soul." Here a sea-faring figure is employed to set forth the peculiar characteristics of the Christian's hope. Hope may be considered as the anchor of the soul in several respects.

A. The anchor is essential to secure the vessel in time of storm and peril. When the Christian is in temptation and distress, hope keeps the soul from throwing away its confidence, and making shipwreck of faith and a good conscience. See Job riding out the storm and singing: "I know that my Redeemer liveth," etc. Paul, waiting his martyrdom: "I know in whom I have believed," etc. (Job 19:25; 2 Tim. 1:12).

B. The anchor is only of service when connected with a good cable. That cable is faith. As this is weak or strong, clear or dark, hope will be lively or depressed. Hope depends for its vigor on a sound and strong faith.

C. The anchor must be employed; otherwise it can be of no service. Neither will hope yield us any advantage unless it be exercised. We must abound in hope, and hope to the end (Heb. 3:6; 6:11; 1 Peter 1:13).

D. The anchor must be cast on good ground. Neither the rock, nor loose yielding sand, will admit the firm, abiding grasp of the anchor. It must be firm ground, or the anchor will slip, and the vessel be driven before the wind. The Christian's anchor rests on Christ's finished work; on His having offered up Himself as the sacrifice, and sprinkled the mercy-seat with His own precious blood: and His ever appearing in the presence of God to make intercession for us. Notice,

III. The Importance of This Hope.

A. It is important to our Christian character. It is as indispensable to the believing soul as the anchor is to the vessel. All God's children are begotten again to this lively hope, etc.

B. It is important to our labors. All must be done in hope. We must sow in hope; pray and wrestle in hope. Hope brightens the eye, energizes the arms, strengthens the shoulders, etc.

C. It is important to our happiness. It is the honey of life, and sweetens every bitter cup. It enlivens our journey. It anticipates future bliss, and assures us of holy pleasure and delight. Notice,

IV. The Certainty of This Hope.

"Both sure and steadfast." This is the very opposite of the hypocrite's hope, which shall perish; and of the hope of the ungodly, which shall be cut off. The Christian's hope cannot fail, unless,

A. The divine veracity fails. He has spoken who is the Truth, and who does not repent, and who cannot change. And this He has not only affirmed by His word, but ratified with His solemn oath (James 1:17; Heb. 6:18). The Christian's hope cannot fail, unless,

B. Christ's precious blood should lose its saving efficacy. By the shedding of that blood He has accomplished our redemption, and secured our salvation. And its efficacy is not only adequate to the deepest stains of human guilt, but its virtue is coexistent with eternity itself (Heb. 5:9). The Christian's hope cannot fail, unless,

C. Christ's presence in heaven and intercession should be unavailing. And when we reflect that He is exalted to the highest dignity there, in His public and official character, that He may see the "travail of His soul, and be satisfied"; therefore, His believing people cannot perish, without Christ being refused His covenanted reward. The Christian's hope is "sure and steadfast," for it rests on Jehovah's word and oath to them, and His word and promise to His Son; and on the continued preciousness of that offering, which possesses infinite and eternal virtue and merit (Isa. 53:10, etc.; Heb. 1:1-13).

Application
1. Let the believer increase in hope, rejoice in hope, until its enrapturing anticipations shall terminate in glorious fruition.
2. Let the hopeless come to the blessed Savior, who will, by the gracious manifestation of Himself, banish darkness from the mind, and despondency and sorrow from the heart. There is, in the gospel, ample ground of hope to all who receive the record God has given of His Son.

CONDENSED FROM JABEZ BURNS

THE HOPE OF THE GOSPEL

1. A good hope (2 Thess. 2:16).

2. A blessed hope (Titus 2:13).

3. A joyful hope (Heb. 3:6; Rom. 5:3).

4. A sure, firm hope (Heb. 6:18).

5. A living or lively hope (1 Peter 1:3).

6. A saving hope (Rom. 8:24).

7. A glorious hope (Col. 1:27).

8. A purifying hope (1 John 3:3).

SELECTED

THE EMPTY TOMB SPEAKS

1 Corinthians 15:1-22; Matthew 28:6

Introduction
- A. Feelings of disciples at empty tomb.
- B. Empty tomb basis of our hope today.
    1. When hope seemed buried, God performed a miracle.
    2. Because He lives we shall live also.

I. Empty Tomb Proves Truthfulness of Prophecy.
- A. Genesis 3:15.
- B. Christ's own words to His disciples.

II. Speaks of the Divinity of Christ.
- A. Both human and divine.
- B. See God through Him.

III. Speaks of His Mission.
- A. Conqueror of death.
- B. Restore life to fallen.

IV. Answers the Question of Job.
- A. "If a man die, shall he live again?"

V. Speaks of a Great Resurrection Morning.
- A. The dawn of a new day.
- B. Dead in Christ rise first.
- C. Very important event.
- D. Christ, the King, our Receptionist.

Conclusion
All hope is secured through the results of the empty tomb.

WATSON

THE GRACIOUS DESIGN OF CHRIST'S COMING

"I am come that they might have life, and that they might have it more abundantly" (John 10:10).

The text contains the good design of Christ's manifestation in the flesh. It is supposed that mankind were dead, and Jesus came expressly to give them life, yea, to give it them more abundantly.

Let us notice, I. The Blessing Referred to and II. The Source of Its Communication.

I. The Blessing Referred to.

"Life." A life suited to man's state and circumstances.

A. A life of justification. In opposition to man's guilty and condemned condition (Rom. 5:18; 8:2).

B. A life of regeneration. In opposition to that spiritual death which has come upon mankind through the fall (John 3:4-8).

C. A life of adoption. In opposition to man's alien estate. By which we become the acknowledged sons and heirs of God (Gal. 4:5).

D. A life of glory everlasting. In opposition to eternal death (John 10:28; Rom. 6:23; 1 John 5:11).

II. The Source of Its Communication.

"I am come that ye might have life," etc. Now Jesus is the great source—the author of life. Jesus—

A. Came to reveal it. It had partially been made known before. But Christ "brought life and immortality to light" (2 Tim. 1:10). He explained all things of importance connected with it. Showed in what it consisted. Made known the way to obtain it, etc.

B. He came to offer it. Hence, His invitations and addresses related to it. He published it, "If any man thirst," etc. "I am the resurrection and the life," etc. He expostulated, "Ye will not come," etc.

C. He came to procure it. And, hence He laid down His life for the world (John 6:51). "He was the propitiation," etc. By His blood He gave a ransom, etc. (1 Tim. 2:6). "He died for us." "Wounded for our transgressions," etc.

D. He came to bestow it. We are justified by His merits. Regenerated by His Spirit. Adopted by His grace. Glorified by Him, and with Him, etc. He is the only communicator either of the life of grace, or of life eternal. Exalted for this purpose, etc.

E.   He came to bestow it more abundantly. An abundance of life exists in Him. Infinite exhaustless life. He has an abundance of life to impart—ever to the whole world—to every creature. Number cannot diminish it. It is offered abundantly. No restriction, or limitation—"More" abundantly; once limited to the Jews, now published to all mankind.

Application

1. Christ has come and brought life near unto us, and we can only obtain it by coming near unto Him. He must be received; and in receiving Him, we receive life.
2. This life must be maintained—perpetuated, by adhering to Christ. His grace and Spirit must preserve and keep us to eternal life.
3. Rejecters of the Gospel. Necessarily exclude themselves from this life, and must, therefore, be the victims of eternal death. The end of ministry is to warn, exhort, etc., that they may flee from the wrath to come.

JABEZ BURNS

HOPE OF THE RESURRECTION

For all who have believed on Christ to the saving of their souls, the hope of the resurrection of the body is:

1.   A comforting hope (Job 19:25, 27; 1 Thess. 4:13, 18).

2.   A satisfying hope (Ps. 17:15).

3.   A sustaining hope (2 Cor. 4:17,18; 5:1, 3).

4.   A lively hope (1 Peter 1:3, 7).

5.   A glorious hope (Rom. 8:18).

6.   A sure hope (John 14:19; Rev. 1:18).

7.   A triumphant hope (Hos. 13:14; 1 Cor. 15:55).

8.   A jubilant hope (Isa. 26:19).

9.   A blessed hope (Rev. 20:6).

10.   A believer's hope (1 John 2:25).

J. ELLIS

THE THREE LOOKS

The eye is the index of the soul, and wherever it turns, there the Spirit may be supposed to be for the time directed; hence God's constant command that we should look. The great facts of redemption are set before us. And they are completed facts; we can add nothing to them by our faith; we can take nothing from them by our unbelief. But they must be appropriated. One opening of the eyelid, and all the beautiful landscape which lay spread out before us instantly becomes an inward experience, imprinted on the camera of our inner consciousness. The three great facts of Christ's redemption are: atonement, advocacy, and advent. And there are three looks corresponding to these:

I. The Backward Look

"Look unto Me, and be ye saved, all the ends of the earth" (Isa. 45:22). The eye is first carried back to the cross, and to Christ's finished work accomplished there. Then, our Redeemer having satisfied the law concerning sin, bids us accept, by our consenting faith, the satisfaction He has made. "Having made peace through the blood of His cross" (Col. 1:20), and therefore, "being justified by faith, we have peace with God through our Lord Jesus Christ" (Rom. 5:1).

II. The Upward Look

"Looking unto Jesus, the author and finisher of our faith; who, for the joy that was set before Him, endured the cross, despising the shame, and is set down at the right hand of the throne of God" (Heb. 12:2). There He is in the place of advocacy, who was before in the place of atonement. Better for the present that He should be there rather than here. The lawyer must be in court if he would conduct the suit of his client; and therefore, Christ has gone "to appear in the presence of God for us" (Heb. 9:24).

III. The Onward Look

"Looking for that blessed hope and the glorious appearing of the great God and our Savior Jesus Christ" (Titus 2:13). This is the true expectation of the believer who waits for full salvation. Our Lord compares Himself to a nobleman going into a far country to receive for Himself a kingdom, and to return. It is for us to wait that return, that we may share that kingdom with Him. "For our conversation is in heaven; from whence, also, we look for the Savior, the Lord Jesus Christ" (Phil. 3:20).   —WATCHWORD, S. P. GORDON

"It doth not yet appear what we shall be: but we know that when He shall appear, we shall be like Him; for we shall see Him as He is" (1 John 3:2).

I. **"It Doth Not Yet Appear What We Shall Be."**

At present we are veiled, and travel through the world incognito.

A. Our Master was not made manifest here below. His glory was veiled in flesh. His Deity was concealed in infirmity. His power was hidden under sorrow and weakness. His riches were buried under poverty and shame.

The world knew Him not, for He was made flesh.

B. We must have an evening before our morning, a schooling before our college, a turning before the music is ready.

C. This is not the time in which to appear in our glory.

> The winter prepares flowers, but does not call them forth.
> The ebb-tide reveals the secrets of the sea,
> but the many of our rivers no gallant ship can then sail.
> To everything there is a season, and this is not the time of glory.

II. **"But We Know That When He Shall Appear."**

A. We speak of our Lord's manifestation without doubt. "We know."

B. Our faith is so assured that it becomes knowledge. He will be manifest upon this earth in person.

III. **"We Shall Be Like Him."**

A. Having a body like His body—sinless, incorruptible, painless, spiritual, clothed with beauty and power, and yet most real and true.

B. Having a soul like His soul—perfect, holy, instructed, developed, strengthened, active, delivered from temptation, conflict, and suffering.

C. Having such dignities and glories as He wears—kings, priests, conquerors, judges, sons of God.

IV. **"We Shall See Him as He Is."**

A. This glorious sight will perfect our likeness.

B. This will be the result of our being like Him.

C. This will be evidence of our being like Him, since none but the pure in heart can see God.

The sight will be ravishing, transforming and transfiguring. The sight will be abiding, and a source of bliss forever.

- Such divine, God-given glimpses into the future reveal to us more than all our thinking. What intense truth, what divine meaning there is in God's creative word: "Let us make man in our image, after our likeness!" To show forth the likeness of the Invisible, to be partaker of the divine nature, to share with God His rule of the universe, is man's destiny. His place is indeed one of unspeakable glory.

A converted blind man once said, "Jesus Christ will be the first person I shall ever see, for my eyes will be opened in heaven."

"You are going to be with Jesus, and to see Him as He is," said a friend to Rowland Hill on his death-bed. "Yes," replied Mr. Hill, with emphasis, "and I shall be like Him; that is the crowning point." —C. H. SPURGEON

CHRIST OUR HOPE

I. Christ Our Hiding Place:
   A. From wrath (John 3:36; Rom. 5:9).
   B. From sin (Acts 13:38, 39; Eph. 1:7).
   C. From temptation (1 Cor. 10:13; 2 Peter 2:9).
   D. From death (1 Cor. 15:54-57; 2 Cor. 5:1).
   E. From judgment (John 3:18; 1 John 3:2,3).

II. Christ's Blood Is:
   A. The sinner's redemption (1 Peter 1:18,19).
   B. The believer's justification (Rom. 5:6-9).
   C. The cleanser from all sin (1 John 1:7).

III. Christ's Coming Again Our Hope (1 John 3:2,3).

IV. In Christ:
   A. We are new creatures (2 Cor. 5:17).
   B. We are sanctified (1 Cor. 1:2).
   C. We have peace (1 Peter 5:14).
   D. We have hope (1 Cor. 15:19).
   E. We have liberty (Gal. 2:4).
   F. We triumph (2 Cor. 2:14).
   G. We shall arise (1 Thess. 4:16).

SELECTED

PROMISES TO HIM WHO OVERCOMES

Revelation 3:12

He Who Overcomes

1. Shall be clothed in white raiment.
2. I will not blot His name out of the Book of Life.
3. I will confess his name before My Father, and before His angels.

He Who Overcomes

1. I will make a pillar in the temple of My God.
2. I will write upon him the name of My God, and the name of the city of My God.
3. And I will write upon him My new name.

To Him Who Overcomes I Will Grant—

To sit with Me in My Throne, even as I also overcame, and am set down with My Father in His throne (Rev. 3:21). "Blessing, and glory, . . . and thanksgiving . . . be unto our God forever and ever" (Rev. 7:21), for "the exceeding riches of His grace" (Eph. 2:7).

SELECTED

THE WALK OF THE CHRISTIAN AND
"THE COMING OF CHRIST"

1. We are to hold fast till He come. The whole truth of God (Rev. 2:20, 23).

2. We are to be steadfast in our service for Christ (1 Cor. 15:58).

3. We are to stand fast in the Lord (Phil. 3:20; 4:1).

4. We are to rejoice in the Lord alway (Phil. 4:4).

5. We are to increase and abound in love one to another that He may establish our hearts unblameable in holiness before God (1 Thess. 3:12,13).

6. We are to seek those things that are above, and set our affection on things above, not on things on the earth; and to mortify our bodies (Col. 3:1-5).

7. We are to fight the good fight of faith, and lay hold on eternal life (1 Tim. 6:12,13,14).

8. We are to preach the Word; be instant in season, out of season; reprove, rebuke, exhort, with all long-suffering and doctrine (2 Tim. 4:2, 8).

9. We are to deny ungodliness and worldly lusts, and to live soberly, righteously, and godly in this present world (Titus 2:12,13).

10. We are to be patient and longsuffering and to establish our hearts (James 5:7,8).

11. We are comforted in regard to our sleeping loved ones, who are with Christ, and as to our speedy reunion with them (1 Thess. 4:13,16).

12. We are to abide in Christ; that we may not be ashamed, and have confidence before Him at His coming (1 John 2:28).

13. We are to hold the Word of His patience and the results to us (Rev. 3:10,11).

14. Those who are elders are to feed the flock of God, and to be as examples to them (1 Peter 5:2).

W. H.

TIME CONSIDERED AND IMPROVED

"But this I say, brethren, the time is short: it remaineth, that both they that have wives be as though they had none" (1 Cor. 7:29-31).

The preciousness of time is universally admitted. Time is that of which life is composed; and so truly rare and valuable is it, that we only possess a single moment of it at once; and our possession of another is a matter of the greatest uncertainty! Let us, then, not only subscribe to the truth of the text, but embody its design in our experience, and exhibit it in our practice. Observe,

I. A Solemn and Momentous Truth Expressed.
"Brethren, the time is short."

There is a sense in which time, in its extended course from the creation to the present period, may be said to be short when viewed through the immutable mind of the Deity, with whom "a thousand years are but as one day"; or when contrasted with the unmeasured and boundless eternity.

But the text evidently refers to the time of human life—the period of our existence upon earth. That which is the limit of man's probation; and the only seed-time in which he can sow for a golden harvest of immortal blessedness.

That our time is short, will appear,

A. When contrasted with the lives of those in the antediluvian world. During that period, there is no account of the death of any in childhood or youth. And many, whose lives are recorded, lived to a very extended age. Adam lived 930 years; Seth lived 912 years; and Methuselah 969 years. How greatly abridged is human existence now! Truly, the time is short. This truth is evident,

B. When viewed through the medium of Scriptural representation. To render the descriptions of the divine word striking and impressive, the language of figure and metaphor is employed. Man's life is spoken of as "a day" (Job 14:6); compared to the flight of an "eagle" (Job 9:26); the "weaver's shuttle"—the "fading leaf"—the "withering grass"—and the "perishing flower" (Job 14:6). It is said to be a vapor. And, to present it in the shortest view possible, it is said to be "as nothing before God" (Ps. 39:5).

C. Our time is short, considered abstractly in itself. It has been computed that a generation of human beings is limited to about thirty-four or thirty-five years. Suppose, however, we reckon on the data given by the Psalmist, that is, threescore years and ten, or fourscore years. What is this, especially when the necessary deductions are made from it?

Childhood and youth will subtract ten years. Sleep about one-third, or twenty years more. And how much must we reckon, as being uselessly, nay, criminally spent, which if possible had better be blotted out?

It will be seen that in this way the man of seventy years really and truly only lives about half that period.

Then observe, the truth of our time being short is especially evident if you consider,

D. The great amount of business that has to be crowded within its narrow limits. Here are the natural, relative, and civil duties of life, besides all the momentous concerns of religion and eternity. Let us notice,

II. The Chain of Practical Inferences the Apostle Deduces from This Truth.

"It remaineth, that both they that have wives be as though they had none," etc.

The inferences all relate to the necessity of moderation in our attachment to, and use of, the things of the present fleeting state. He infers,

A. As to the endearing ties of social life. "They that have wives," etc. The inference is alike applicable to parents, children, friends, etc. These we are to love, and do them all the good in our power. But we are not to idolize them; not reckon upon their continuance; we hold them by a very brittle and tender thread. Behold Abraham weeping over the remains of Sarah; Jacob over Rachel; Rachel refusing to be comforted, etc. He infers,

B. As to the sorrows of life. "And they that weep as though they wept not." This world is truly a valley of tears! Many causes. But still, the Christian should not sorrow excessively. He is not a permanent resident in it. But he infers, also,

C. As to the joy of time. "They that rejoice, as though they rejoiced not." The Christian has his joys, as well as his griefs. It is both his duty and privilege to rejoice in the Lord. But these must be moderated. "Rejoice with trembling." Not to be too much elated on this side Canaan.

D. As to the business of this life. "They that buy, as though they possessed not." Not to be too deeply immersed in worldly concerns. Not to be too anxious about the riches of time. Not to idolize created good. Not to be absorbed in our worldly possessions. If riches increase, not to set our hearts upon them. The rich fool. He infers,

E. As to the proper use of the world. "They that use this world, as not abusing it." To use the world is, with thankfulness to receive God's creatures, and to apply them to their intended design with moderation and prayer. To abuse it, is to pervert it—to waste it—to apply it to worthless and criminal purposes. To use it is to act with it, and lay it out as stewards who must give a full and solemn account for its possession. To use it as a traveler uses the inn, where he stops for the night; or as the passenger, who accommodates himself to the vessel till he reaches the destined port. Use it as the pilgrim does his staff, from which he derives assistance, till he arrives at the city of his habitation. Then notice,

III. The Impressive and Forcible Application of This Truth.

"For the fashion of this world passeth away." All the gaudy scenery of this world is perpetually changing, and, like some pompous gorgeous procession, passes away. Its riches, honors, power, all pass away. Its cities and empires pass away. The same applies to beauty, health, strength, and life itself; for they all pass away. The world itself is groaning with age; and speedily shall lose its present fashion, and be burned up.

Application

1. Highly prize and value time.
2. Wisely expend it.
3. Daily improve it.
4. Live for eternity; by living in Christ—and to Christ—and for Christ.
5. Be looking for the mercy of our Lord Jesus Christ to eternal life.

JABEZ BURNS

THE MOMENTOUS WORD

"Eternity" (Isa. 57:15).

This all-momentous word is only to be found once in the whole of the inspired pages. Yet how unconcernedly we often use it. It is utterly incomprehensible. No finite mind can grasp it. We are, however, intimately and indissolubly connected with it. It behooves us, therefore, to do all we can to understand as much of it as possible.

Let us inquire, then,

I. **What We Understand by "Eternity."**

Eternity is duration without limits. As such it has neither beginning nor end. In this sense it is only applicable to God, for Jehovah is alone truly and properly eternal. Other beings, as angels and men, have a sort of prospective eternity, are immortal, and will exist forever, but as they were not always in existence, they are not strictly eternal. Eternity has been likened to a ring, which has no beginning or end. Eternity is not unaptly said to resemble the scene presented to the mariner when out at sea, when he looks abroad in every direction, and perceives nothing but the waters of the mighty ocean. Eternity necessarily includes duration beyond all that figures can describe or ideas conceive. There are a certain number of grains of sand on the seashore; a certain number of drops in the mighty ocean; a certain number of blades of grass, and leaves upon the trees; and, were myriads of ages to pass between the annihilation of each of these, there would finally cease to be a grain of sand, etc. But eternity would then be no nearer its termination than at the first, and would still be duration without limits. Let us, then,

II. **Consider Some Things Directly Connected with It.**

A. The existence of man shall be eternal. The soul shall never die; and the deceased body shall be raised again to immortality and endless life.

B. The believer's happiness will be eternal. Hence we read of eternal redemption and eternal salvation (Heb. 5:9, and 9:12). Eternal weight of glory (2 Cor. 4:17). Eternal inheritance (Heb. 9:15). Eternal life, etc. (John 6:54, and 10:28; Rom. 6:23).

C. The sinner's misery will be eternal. Hence we read of eternal damnation (Matt. 3:29); eternal fire (Jude 7). Also we read of everlasting punishment (Matt. 25:46); everlasting destruction (2 Thess. 1:9). Let us, then,

III. Make Some Useful Application of It.
The subject should lead us,

A. To high and sublime views of Deity. He, and He only, inhabits eternity. How great and unsearchable is God! We see,

B. The dignity and preciousness of man. A candidate for eternity; an immortal deathless being. "What shall it profit a man," etc.

C. The evanescence and shortness of time. A vapor, shadow, thing of naught, etc.

D. The vast importance of life. Time of escape from eternal wrath; of preparation for glory; only seed-time for a harvest of blessedness or woe. "Redeeming the time," etc.

E. The solemnity of death. The outlet of life! The gate of eternity! Passage to heaven or to hell!

Let the subject of eternity daily impress our minds; let us do everything in reference to eternity—preach, hear, pray, live, etc. How necessary to be serious, wise, sincere, watchful, etc.

JABEZ BURNS

THE LORD'S SUPPER A MEMORIAL 'TILL HE COME

1 Corinthians 11:26

1. In remembrance of Me—from the Cross to glory (Luke 22:19; 24:26).

2. Me, the crucified One, who His own self bare our sins in His own body on the tree (1 Peter 2:24).

3. Me, the risen One. He was raised . . . for our justification (Rom. 4:25).

4. Me, the ascended One, now in the presence of God for us (Heb. 9:24; 1:3).

5. Me, the living One. He ever liveth to make intercession for us (Heb. 7:25).

6. Me, the coming One. I will come again and receive you unto Myself (John 14:3; Heb. 9:28).

HANDFULS OF HELP

THE DAY OF SALVATION

"Behold, now is the day of salvation" (2 Cor. 6:2).

Subject of the text; the highest and most important that can engage our attention; that on which the wisdom, power, and goodness of Deity have been most prominently displayed; that which angels contemplate with delight; and that which is identified with all our hopes of solid happiness, either in this life, or that which is to come. Let us consider the passage as it stands before us.

I. Salvation, II. Day of Salvation and III. The Attention It Demands from Us. "Behold, now is the day of salvation."

I. Salvation

Salvation implies misery, or danger, or both of them; and includes deliverance from them. Man's state is both miserable and dangerous. He is a rebel, outlawed, under sentence of death. In addition to which, he is wretched, poor, diseased, ready to perish. His condition is one of extreme wretchedness and imminent peril.

Salvation provides deliverance from the danger, and restoration from the misery. It announces pardon for his crimes, and a balm for all his illnesses.

This salvation—which is the product of divine love, the effect of the Redeemer's death, and the work of the Holy Spirit, and which is received by faith—is,

A. Perfect in its nature. It is adapted to our state, and commensurate with all our misery and crimes. It embraces both the body and the soul.

B. Present in its application. Revealed now, offered now, must be received now.

C. Universal in its extent. "Whosoever will, may come," etc. It is not God's will that any should perish, etc. Christ died for the world (John 3:16; 1 John 2:2). And the gospel is to be preached through all the world to every creature (Mark 16:16).

D. Free in its communication. Not bestowed in the way of human merit, but without money and without price (Isa. 55:1, etc.).

E. Eternal in its duration. Which shall endure forever (2 Tim. 2:10; Heb. 5:9; 1 Peter 5:10; John 3:15; 10:28; Rom. 6:23).

II. Day of Salvation

This may refer generally to the world, or specially to man. Let us consider it,

A. Generally to the world. It includes the whole space of time, from the first promise to the end of the gospel age. First promise; the glimmering of light. Patriarchal age; the daybreak. Prophetical era; the morning. Christ's incarnation; the rising of the Sun of Righteousness, etc. Ours is necessarily the evening of this day.

B. Specially to man. Then it is the period of human life, a short, uncertain period—only time of light and exercise, which terminates in the night of death, and the darkness of the grave (Eccl. 9:10).

III. The Attention It Demands

A. It has a claim upon our examination. What are we doing? How do we stand in reference to God, salvation, death, and eternity? It has a claim,

B. Upon our consideration. "O that they were wise, that they knew this," etc. (Deut. 32:29; Ps. 1:22; Isa. 1:3; Ezek. 12:3; Hag. 1:5).

C. Upon our faith. Now we have the cross, the gospel, the instruction, the warrant, the promise—"He that believeth shall be saved."

D. Upon our diligence. What have we to do? Soul to save—generation work—heaven to gain—to provide for eternity, etc. "Give diligence to make your calling and election sure" (2 Peter 1:10; 3:14).

Application

1. Let us be earnest in reference to this salvation ourselves. And,
2. Recommend it to the attention of all around us.

> "Point sinners to the Savior's blood,
> And cry, Behold the way to God."

JABEZ BURNS

ENTRANCE AND EXCLUSION

"They that were ready went in with Him to the marriage: and the door was shut" (Matt. 25:10).

During the waiting period, the virgins seemed much alike, even as at this day one can hardly discern the false professor from the true.

When the midnight cry was heard the difference began to appear, as it will do when the Second Advent approaches.

I. **The Ready, and Their Entrance.**
   A. What is this readiness? "They that were ready."
      It is not a fruit of nature.
      It must be a work of grace.
      It mainly consists in a secret work wrought in us.
      In being reconciled to God by the death of His Son.
      In being regenerated, and so made meet for glory.
      In being anointed with the Spirit, and fitted for holy service.
   B. What is this entrance?
      Immediate. "They that were ready went in."
      No sooner was the Bridegroom come, than they went in.
         Love allows no delays.
      Intimate. They "went in with Him."
      Joyous. They went in with Him "to the marriage."

II. **The Unready, and Their Exclusion.**
   A. What is this unreadiness?
      It was the absence of a secret essential; but that absence
         was consistent with much apparent preparation.
      These persons had the name and character of virgins.
      They had the lamps or torches of true bridesmaids.
      They were companions of the true virgins.
      They acted like the true; in their virtues and in their faults.
      They awakened as the true did, startled by the same cry.
      They prayed also, after a fashion—"give us of your oil."
      Yet were they never ready to enter in with the King.
      They had no heart-care to be found ready, hence flaming
         external lamps, but no hidden internal oil.
   B. What is this exclusion?
      It was universal to all who were not ready.

It was complete: "the door was shut"—shut for those without quite assuredly as for those within.

It was just; for they were not ready, and so slighted the King. It was final. Since the fatal news that the door was shut, no news has come that it has been opened, or that it ever will be.

- A lady who heard Whitefield, in Scotland, preach upon the words, "And the door was shut," being placed near two dashing young men, but at a considerable distance from the pulpit, witnessed their mirth; and overheard one to say, in a low tone, to the other, "Well, what if the door be shut? Another will open." Thus they turned off the solemnity of the text.

  Mr. Whitefield had not proceeded far when he said, "It is possible there may be some careless, trifling person here today, who may ward off the force of this impressive subject by lightly thinking, 'What matter if the door be shut? Another will open.'" The two young men were paralyzed, and looked at each other. Mr. Whitefield proceeded: "Yes; another will open. And I will tell you what door it will be: it will be the door of the bottomless pit!—the door of hell!—the door which conceals from the eyes of angels the horrors of damnation!"—C. H. SPURGEON

THE TWO WAITINGS

Luke 8:40

The introduction to the text is briefly this: Jesus had been making a short excursion by sea; the storm; among the Gadarenes; return home; welcome back.

I. The One Awaited

    A. He was One who was worth waiting for.

Were you ever in a peach orchard and undertook to choose a ripe peach? So men get "left" in life; but not with Jesus.

    B. He was One who never disappointed.

Bernard del Carpio deceived by his king; Jesus never made a promise that He didn't keep.

    C. He was One who was apt to come when least expected.

The story of the Wise and Foolish Virgins. Who expected Jesus when He was born in Bethlehem?

II. Those Who Were Waiting

    A. Among them were some anxious ones.

Possibly Jairus was there. The woman who touched His robe may have been there.

    B. Among them were some curious ones.

    C. Among them were some hostile ones.

Classification of Indians. "Hostiles," "Friendlies." The Chief Priests, Scribes and Pharisees as a body were always hostile.

III. What the Crowd Was Doing

    A. A picture rises before my imagination!

We are on the lakeshore, just outside Capernaum; an immense throng is standing there and looking out over the sea. It is dawn, the hills of Moab, the breeze, the mist, a fishing boat, in the bow is Jesus.

    B. How they all waited.

They were full of ardent, glowing expectancy. In religious waiting, there is at times indifferences, again, half-heartedness, and still again a sort of despair.

    C. What came of this waiting?

The healing of the sick woman; the raising of Jairus' daughter.

IV. This Is a Gospel Parable for Today
   A. It is the same mighty Jesus who is being waited for today!
   B. It is the same mixed crowd that is waiting for Him!

All men are waiting for Jesus, though so many don't know what they are waiting for. The pleasure-seekers, money-makers, power-lovers, the restless all seeking the satisfaction. He alone, etc. The heathen world, the Messiah-craze.

   C. It is the same varied result from this waiting!

SKETCHES OF REVIVAL SERMONS

THE TEN VIRGINS

Matthew 25:1-13

The Message

That some are wise and some are foolish in their attitude toward Christ. That the consequences of foolishness will be fatal.

   I. Introduction. Jesus made use of familiar incidents, such as wedding feasts, to teach spiritual lessons. We must try to get the teaching, but not to go beyond it, imagining comparisons which Jesus does not make.

   II. An Event About to Happen. A wedding—an occasion of festivity and happiness. To share in such rejoicing it was worth while to wait, even though the bridegroom should tarry. We wait a more glorious moment, the coming of the Savior for His Church.

   III. A Privilege Free to All. In the parable, to have part in the rejoicing at the wedding; today, to have part in heavenly joys.

   IV. A Necessary Preparation. Then, lamps lighted, and today—What? The light of the Gospel shining in our heart and life. Does the hearer feel the lack of anything in his life in order to be able to meet the heavenly Bridegroom?

   V. The Application is made by the Lord Himself. "Watch therefore, for ye know neither the day nor the hour wherein the Son of Man cometh."

The Second Coming of Christ was never so near as now. Now knowing the day, we should always be prepared. Let us think whether we lack any necessary preparation to meet with Christ.

SELECTED

THE SIGNS OF THE END

Daniel 12:6

I. The Signs of the End, in the World.
   A. Progress of false religion.
   B. A rampant infidelity.
   C. Persecution of the good.
   D. Unbelief of the world.

II. Signs in the Church.
   A. Increased activities—Missions.
   B. Quickened zeal—Personal effort.

SELECTED

THE LAST DAYS

Let us consider how "the last days" are defined and described in the Scripture, both Old and New Testaments:

I. Defined:
   A. Began with manifestation of Christ (1 Peter 1:19,20).
   B. Continued through ministry of Christ (Heb. 1:2).
   C. Were in the days of John (1 John 2:18).
   D. To last to the millennial age (Isa. 2:2-4).

II. Described:
   A. Perilous times (2 Tim. 3:1-5).
   B. Mockers (Jude 18,19).
   C. Scoffers (2 Peter 3:3).
   D. Antichrists and antichrist (1 John 2:18).
   E. Indignation accomplished (Dan. 8:19-25).
   F. Spirit poured out, signs in heaven (Acts 2:17-21).
   G. Salvation of the saints (1 Peter 1:5).
   H. Jerusalem established, world blessed (Isa. 2:2-4; Mic. 4:1-4).

H. W. FROST

READY FOR THE GREAT DAY OF THE LORD

Zephaniah 1:14-18

Introduction

To be taken directly from the text. We need to be ready. "Therefore be ye ready . . ." (Matt. 24:44).

I. **Sinner's Readiness:**

A. Pulling them out of the fire (Jude 23). "Lake which burneth . . ." (Rev. 21:8). Sinners are doomed unless they repent before the day of the Lord.

B. How great a matter a little fire kindleth (James 3:6). Oil well explosion, etc.

C. "What is a man profited if he shall gain the whole world and lose his own soul?" (Matt. 16:26).

II. **Believer's Readiness. Preparation preceded readiness:**

A. No water until ditches dug (2 Kings 3:16,17).

B. No oil until vessels were gathered (2 Kings 4:3,4).

C. No healing until the leper had dipped in the muddy Jordan river (2 Kings 5:10).

D. No resurrection until the stone was removed (John 11:39).

III. **Signs of His Coming.** "When ye see these things. . . ."

A. Increase of knowledge (Dan. 12:4).

B. Many shall run to and fro (Dan. 12:4).

C. Automobiles, planes, etc. (Nah. 2:3,4).

D. Dislike of the truth (2 Tim. 4:3,4; 2:15).

E. Lovers of selves more than God (2 Tim. 3:2).

F. Disobedience of children (2 Tim. 3:2). Loss of natural affection (2 Tim. 3:3).

G. Love of pleasure (2 Tim. 3:4).

H. False Christs (Matt. 24:12).

I. Abounding in iniquity (Matt. 24:12).

J. Wars, famines, pestilence, earthquakes (Matt. 24).

"Watch ye therefore: for ye know not at what hour the Lord doth come." Two grinding. Two in a field. As in the days of Noe.

"As the lightning cometh . . ." (Matt. 24:27).

"Blessed is the servant whom His Master shall find so doing." Amen. SELECTED

THE ANTICHRIST

I. The Spirit of Antichrist Is Already in the World:
- A. Now already is it in the world (1 John 4:3).
- B. Even now are there many (1 John 2:18).
- C. This is a deceiver and an antichrist (2 John 7).
- D. He is the antichrist that denies the Father and the Son (1 John 2:22).

II. There Is a Final Antichrist Who Is Yet to Come:
- A. Whereof you have heard that it should come (1 John 4:3).
- B. You have heard that antichrist shall come (1 John 2:18).
- C. That man of sin shall be revealed (2 Thess. 2:3).

III. The Antichrist Is Not a System, But a Person:
- A. Antichrist shall come (1 John 2:18).
- B. He magnified himself (Dan. 8:11).
- C. That man of sin shall be revealed, the son of perdition (2 Thess. 2:3).

IV. When Antichrist Is to Be Revealed:
- A. At the last time (1 John 2:18).
- B. In the last days (Dan. 8:13-25).
- C. At the end-time, when Christ comes (2 Thess. 2:8; Rev. 19:19,20).

V. Where Antichrist Is to Arise:
- A. From the old world (the "sea" is the Mediterranean) (Rev. 13:1).
- B. From the locality where stood the Grecian kingdom (Dan. 8:21-23).

VI. What Antichrist's Character Is to Be:
- A. A denier of the Father and the Son (1 John 2:22).
- B. A denier of Christ (1 John 4:2; 2 John 7).
- C. A liar, and, the lie (1 John 2:22; 2 Thess. 2:11).
- D. That Wicked One (2 Thess. 2:8).
- E. The man of sin and son of perdition (2 Thess. 2:3).
- F. A deceiver (Dan. 11:32; 2 Thess. 2:9,10).
- G. A blasphemer (Dan. 7:25; 8:11; 11:36,37; Rev. 13:5,6; 2 Thess. 2:3,4).

H. A miracle worker (Dan. 8:23-25; 2 Thess. 2:9,10; Rev. 13:12-15).

I. Satan's masterpiece (2 Thess. 2:9; Rev. 13:4-8).

VII. What Antichrist's Work Will Be:

A. He will be a king (Dan. 7:24; 8:23; Rev. 17:10-12).

B. He will assume great power:

1. Politically (Dan. 7:8, 25; 8:23,24; Rev. 13:1,2 ; 17:12, 17; Dan. 11:41-44).

2. Commercially (Dan. 8:25; Rev. 13:16,17).

3. Religiously (Rev. 17:1-11, 15).

C. He will corrupt many by prosperity (Dan. 8:25, margin).

D. He will carry on great wars (Dan. 7:20-25; 11:21-45; Rev. 13:2-4).

E. He will make a covenant with the Jews and restore to them their land and religion (Dan. 9:27; Matt. 24:15,16).

F. He will break this covenant (Dan. 11:28-31; 9:27; 8:11).

G. He will fight against the saints and destroy many (Dan. 7:25; 8:24; Rev. 13:7, 15; 12:13-17; Matt. 24:15-22).

H. He will attempt battle against Christ (Rev. 17:13,14; 19:19).

VIII. What Antichrist's End Will Be:

A. The kings of the south and north will war with him (Dan. 11:40-45).

B. Christ and His armies will go out against him (Rev. 19:11-19).

C. Antichrist will come to his end (Dan. 7:25,26; Rev. 17:17).

D. He will be destroyed (Dan. 7:26; 8:25; 9:27, R.V.; 2 Thess. 2:8,9).

E. He will be cast alive into the lake of fire:

1. Son of perdition (2 Thess. 2:3).

2. Goes into perdition (Rev. 17:11).

3. Cast into the lake of fire (Rev. 19:19,20).

H. W. FROST

PREPARE YE THE WAY

Matthew 3:3

Introduction

Though John's ministry has come and gone, in a sense this command is applicable to every generation.

I. **Consider Signs That Indicate His Kingdom Is at Hand:**

    A. The spirit of national revival.

    B. The turning to Christ and the church of many well-known leaders in all walks of life.

    C. The feeling of expectancy in the church.

II. **How May We Prepare the Way of the Lord?**

    A. Step number One: "Repent ye" (v. 12).

        1. By "acknowledging our sin" (Rom. 3:10).

        2. By "confessing our sin" (1 John 1:9).

        3. By "turning away from sin" (Repentance).

        4. By "forsaking sin" (Quit the sin business).

III. **By Obedience to His Commands:**

    A. Following Christ in baptism (v. 6).

    B. Seeking "Christ's Baptism," of the Holy Spirit (v. 11).

    C. Walking in all the light (1 John 1:7).

IV. **By Dedicating Our Talents to the Lord:**

    A. Faithfulness to God's house.

    B. Paying of our tithes in its support.

    C. Loyalty and support for all her auxiliaries.

V. **By a Life of Prayer for Christ's Return:**

    A. Seeking the salvation of the lost.

    B. And praying, "Even so, come, Lord Jesus."

SELECTED

THE ADVENT IN THE THESSALONIAN EPISTLES

"The coming of our Lord Jesus Christ" (1 Thess. 5:23).

There are three "mountain peaks" or comings in the New Testament: the First coming of Christ, the coming of the Holy Spirit, and the Second coming of Christ. Each is vitally important and should have due attention. The third one of these is often neglected, even though it is mentioned 300 times in the New Testament. It is often thought that the Second Coming is impractical and has no bearing on life, and this in spite of 1 John 3:3 and 2 Peter 3:11,14. But—

"There is nothing," says Dean Alford, "that so much takes a man out of himself; nothing that so much raises and widens his thoughts and sympathies; nothing that so much purifies and elevates his hopes, as this preparation for the coming of the Lord.

Of the earliest Epistles of Paul, seven are addressed to churches. These may be divided into four groups: those which have as their primary purpose: (1) doctrinal foundation; (2) church life; (3) Christian experience; and (4) the coming of the Lord. In this fourth group are the two epistles to the Thessalonians, of which every chapter but one treats of the Second Coming and even that includes it indirectly. The Lord's coming is shown to imply:

I. Hope (1 Thess. 1:3, 10).
    A. Essential part of Christian life: all three, faith, hope and love, mentioned (v. 3).
    B. Essential part of evidence proving original Gospel (v. 10).

II. Work (1 Thess. 2:17-19).
    A. Present love of soul-winner (vv. 17,18).
    B. Future prospect: association, presentation (v. 19).

III. Holiness (1 Thess. 3:12,13).
    Heart in Scripture includes mind, emotion and will, i.e., whole personality.
    A. What? "Unblameable in holiness"—then.
        "Stablished in love"—now.
    B. Where? "Before God."
    C. When? "At the coming of our Lord Jesus Christ."

IV. Comfort (1 Thess. 4:13-18).

A. Problem (v. 13).
B. Solution (v. 14).
C. Revelation (vv. 15-17).
D. Consolation (v. 18).

V. **Character (1 Thess. 5:1-28).**
A. Edification (vv. 1-11).
"You" (vv. 1,2); "they" (v. 3); "we" (v. 5); therefore, "let us" (vv. 6-8); "be sober" (vv. 6, 8); "in order to 'edify'" (v. 11).
B. Preservation (vv. 12-14).
1. Aspects of life (vv. 12-22).
2. Anticipation of future (v. 23).
3. Assurance of fulfillment (v. 24).
4. Therefore, let us be alert, helpful, thorough.

VI. **Vindication (2 Thess. 1:1-12).**
A. Rest after persecution (vv. 6,7).
B. Glory after opposition (v. 10).

VII. **Steadfastness (2 Thess. 2:1-17).**
A. Information (vv. 1-12).
B. Exhortation (vv. 13-17).

VIII. **Patience (2 Thess. 3:1-18).**
Cf. verse 5 with James 5:8.

Conclusion
Christ has come—Bethlehem
Christ is coming—Pentecost
Christ will come—Olivet

W. H. GRIFFITH THOMAS

HIS COMING AGAIN

I. In Person (John 14:1-3; 1 Thess. 4:16).

II. The Reason (John 14:3).
    To receive you unto Myself. The living and dead saints (1 Cor.
    15:51,52; 1 Thess. 4:15-17).
    A. This is the first resurrection (Rev. 20:5,6).
    B. Resurrection of the just (Luke 14:14).
    C. Resurrection from the among the dead (Phil. 3:11).
    D.Called. The day of Redemption (Eph. 4:30; 1:13,14; Rom.
      8:23).

III. The Attitude.
    A. Groaning (Rom. 8:23).
    B. Looking (Titus 2:13; Heb. 9:28; Phil. 3:19, 21).
    C. Waiting (1 Thess. 1:10; 2 Thess. 3:5; 1 Cor. 1:7,8).
    D. Watching (Mark 13:35; Luke 12:37; 1 Thess. 5:2, 6).
    E. Loving (2 Tim. 4:8; 1 Peter 5:4).

IV. Practical Aspect.
    A. Separation (1 John 3:2,3; Phil. 3:20).
    B. Self-denial (Col. 3:4,5).
    C. Occupation (Luke 19:11-13).
    D. Holiness (2 Peter 3:11-14).
    E. Time of rejoicing (1 Peter 1:7; 1 Thess. 2:19).
    F. In glory (Col. 3:14; Rom. 8:18).
    G. Like Him (1 John 3:2; Ps. 17:15).

V. When Shall These Things Be? (Mark 13:32-37; 2 Peter 3:10;
    Rev. 16:15; Matt. 24:27, 37,38; Luke 17:26, 29; 1 Thess. 5:1-
    3; Matt. 24:44; Rev. 22:7, 12, 20).

VI. What It Means to the Unsaved (Jude 14,15; Rev. 1:7;
    19:11-14; 7:15-17; 20:11-15; John 5:27; Acts 17:31; 10:42; 2
    Thess. 1:7,8,9; Isa. 26:21; 63:3-6; Jer. 5:31).

SELECTED

DEATH AND THE LORD'S COMING CONTRASTED

I. Death is the penalty of sin, but the Lord's coming delivers from sin and penalty (Rom. 6:23; 1 Thess. 4:17).

II. Thoughts and experiences of the one, painful; of the other, delightful (John 11:31; Titus 2:13).

III. In one event we look downward and weep; in the other, upward and rejoice (John 11:35; Phil. 2:16).

IV. In one the body is sown in corruption and dishonor; in the other, it is raised incorruptible and in glory (1 Cor. 15:42,43).

V. In one event we were unclothed; in the other, clothed upon (2 Cor. 5:4).

VI. In one a sad separation of friends; in the other, a glad reunion (Ezek. 24:16; 1 Thess 4:13,14).

VII. We enter into rest at death, but we are crowned at the Lord's coming (1 Thess. 4:13; 2 Tim. 4:8).

VIII. Death comes as our great enemy; Christ as our great friend (1 Cor. 15:36; Prov. 18:24).

IX. Death is the king of terrors; Christ is the king of glory (Job 18:14; Ps. 24:7).

X. Satan has the power of death; Christ is the Prince of Life (Heb. 2:14; Acts 3:15).

XI. In one event we depart to be with Christ; in the other, He comes to us (Phil 1:23; John 14:3).

XII. Christ and the Apostles never commanded saints to watch for death, but repeatedly to await the Lord's coming (1 Cor. 15:51; Matt. 25:13).

We may see here that the frequently assumed resemblance between these two events is strikingly unscriptural and false.

We should also understand that the practice of applying parables, instructions, and exhortations to death, which we know were expressly spoken of the Lord's coming, is a false and dangerous method of interpretation (Jer. 23:28; Rev. 22:18,19).

E. P. Marvin

43

CHRIST'S SECOND COMING AND DEATH

Christ's coming and death are the very opposite of each other, and one never stands for the other in Scripture.

1. Death is an enemy (1 Cor. 15:26).
   Coming of Christ is the coming of a friend.

2. Death the penalty for sin (Rom. 6:23).
   Coming of Christ will deliver us forever from sin and its penalty.

3. Death is the king of terrors (Job 18:14).
   We look for the King of kings and Lord of lords.

4. Death is sorrowful and painful (Ps. 18:4; 116:3).
   Christ's coming is a happy event.

5. Death is cruel separation (Gen. 37:35; John 11:31).
   Christ's coming is glad reunion (1 Thess. 4:16,17).

6. Death casts unto a grave of corruption (1 Cor. 15:42, 43).
   Christ's coming lifts us from the grave.

7. Death has lorded over all (Rom. 5:17; Heb. 9:27).
   Coming of Christ does away with death of His people.
   "Death is swallowed up in victory."

JAMES SPINK

WITH CHRIST IN GLORY

Philippians 1:23

I. **What Is It to Be with Christ?**
   A. To behold His presence.
   B. To share His glory.
   C. To enjoy His communion.

II. **Why Is It Far Better?**
   A. Better bodies.
   B. Better souls.
   C. Better company.
   D. Better employment.
   E. Better enjoyment.
   F. Better honors.

SELECTED

THE OUTCOME OF WAITING FOR CHRIST

1. Unceasing **Watchfulness**.
   "Shall find watching" (Luke 12:37).
2. Unswerving **Fidelity**.
   "To every man his work" (Mark 13:34).
3. Unwearied **Patience**.
   "Be ye also patient" (James 5:8).
4. Unflinching **Obedience**.
   "Shall find so doing" (Matt. 24:46).
5. Increasing **Holiness**.
   "Unblameable in holiness" (1 Thess. 3:13).
6. Unfailing **Comfort**.
   "Comfort one another" (1 Thess. 4:18).
7. Unending **Work**.
   "Occupy, till I come" (Luke 19:13).

—SELECTED

THE CHRISTIAN'S NEW BODY

1. It will be **like Christ's**.
   "Like unto His own glorious body" (Phil. 3:21).

2. It will be **redeemed**.
   "The redemption of the body" (Rom. 8:23).

3. It will be **eternal**.
   "Eternal in the heavens" (2 Cor. 5:1).

4. It will be **incorruptible**.
   "Raised in incorruption" (1 Cor. 15:42).

5. It will be **glorious**.
   "Raise in glory" (1 Cor. 15:43).

6. It will be **powerful**.
   "Raised in power" (1 Cor. 15:43).

7. It will be **spiritual**.
   "A spiritual body" (1 Cor. 15:44).

SELECTED

THE DAY OF THE LORD

Job 19:25

I. Appointed a Day (Acts 17:31).
    A. Day is near—a cloudy day (Ezek. 30:3).
    B. Day of darkness—not light (Amos 5:18).
    C. Day of destruction (Isa. 13:6, 9, 13).
    D. Of darkness and gloom (Joel 1:15).
    E. Great and very terrible (Joel 2:11).
    F. Wonders in heaven and earth (Joel 2:30,31).
    G. Darkness—smoke—fire (Joel 2:30,31).

II. Near at Hand (Zeph. 1:14).
    A. Of wrath—of the trumpet (Zeph. 1:15-18).
    B. Of the Lord's anger (Zeph. 2:2,3).
    C. Who may abide the day (Mal. 3:2).
    D. Shall burn as an oven (Matt. 4:1).
    E. Wonderful chapter (Zech. 14).

III. How Shall Christ Come?
    A. In the glory of His Father (Matt. 16:27).
    B. With angels (Matt. 24:30).
    C. With power and great glory (Matt. 24:31).
    D. Shall sit on His throne (Matt. 26:31).
    E. On the right hand of power (Matt. 26:31).
    F. In the clouds of Heaven (Matt. 26:64).
    G. With the voice of the archangel, and the trump of God (1 Thess. 4:16,17).
    H. With ten thousand saints (Jude 1:14,15).

IV. When?
    A. As a thief in the night (1 Thess. 5:1,2).
    B. Heaven shall pass away (2 Peter 3:10-12).
    C. Draweth nigh (James 5:7,8).
    D. Comes quickly (Rev. 22:12, 17, 20).
    E. Visions of it (Rev. 6:12-17; Rev. 20:11-15).
    F. Exhortations (2 Cor. 5:10,11; 1 Cor. 3:8; 2 Thess. 1:6-9; 2 Tim. 4:1-8; Heb. 9:27,28; 1 Peter 4:5, 7, 17,18; 1 Peter 5:4; 1 John 4:17).

SELECTED

THE COMING CHRIST

I. Christ's Second Coming Will Be:
   A. Personal:
      1. I will come (John 14:3,4).
      2. This same Jesus (Acts 1:10,11).
      3. Behold He cometh (Rev. 1:7).
   B. Literal:
      1. In like manner as He went (Acts 1:10,11).
      2. Into the air (1 Thess. 4:16,17).
      3. To Olivet, from whence He ascended (Acts 1:11,12, with Zech. 14:1-4).
   C. Visible:
      1. To the Church (Heb. 9:28).
      2. To the Jews (Rev. 1:7).
      3. To the entire world (Rev. 1:7).
   D. Sudden:
      1. In a moment (1 Cor. 15:51,52).
      2. Like the flash of lightning (Matt. 24:27).
   E. Unexpected:
      1. Men will be sleeping and doubting (Matt. 24:48-51).
      2. As a thief comes (Rev. 16:15; 1 Thess. 5:2,3).
   F. Glorious:
      1. In God's glory (Matt. 16:27).
      2. In the glory of the saints (Col. 3:4).
      3. In the glory of the angels (Matt. 25:31).

II. Christ Will Come:
   A. As King.
      1. A King shall reign (Isa. 32:1).
      2. To rule over the nations (Zech. 14:16).
      3. As King of kings (Ps. 72:1-11; Rev. 19:16).
   B. To establish the millennium:
      1. He will then subdue evil (2 Thess. 2:8; Rev. 19:20).
      2. The reign of the thousand years (Rev. 20:1-6).

III. His Coming Will Be Blessed:
   A. A time of union with Christ (1 Thess. 4:16,17).
   B. Time of reunion among the Christians (1 Thess. 4:13, 17).
   C. Time of rewarding (1 Cor. 4:5; Rev. 11:15, 18).

D. Time of triumph (Rev. 19:11-14; 20:4-6).
E. Evil will be destroyed (Matt. 25:31).
F. Universal peace shall be set up (Ps. 72:1-7).
G. A time of universal blessing (Acts 15:16,17).

IV. His Coming Is Imminent:
A. The time is at hand (Rev. 1:3).
B. The Lord is at hand (Phil. 4:5).
C. He will not tarry (Heb. 10:36,37).
D. He cometh quickly (Rev. 22:7, 12, 20).

SELECTED

THREEFOLD OBJECT OF THE LORD'S COMING

Coming to Receive (Matt. 25:6).
Coming to Reckon (Matt. 25:19).
Coming to Judge (Matt. 25:31).

SELECTED

THE LORD'S COMING

1 Thessalonians 4:13-18; 5:1-6

This is a subject full of vital interest for these last days. Let us note carefully the following facts:

I. **That the Lord Will Come Again: Himself Shall Descend (v. 16).**
    This is not the coming of death, nor is it the coming of the Holy Spirit. "This same Jesus . . ." (Acts 1:11).

II. **That Those Who Sleep in Jesus Will Come with Him (v. 14).**
    What a company! What a reunion!

III. **That Those Who Are Alive When He Comes Shall Not Go Before Those Who Are Asleep (v. 15).**
    Hence those who have died in the Lord shall lose nothing by it, and those who remain alive at His coming shall be spared the pain of dying, but shall not precede the former.

IV. **That the Dead in Christ Shall Rise First (v. 16).**
    It will only be they "that are Christ's" at His coming (1 Cor. 15:23). Blessed and holy is He that hath part in the first resurrection (Rev. 20:6).

V. **That All Shall Be Caught Up Together (v. 17).**
    The dead raised and the living changed in a moment, in the twinkling of an eye (1 Cor. 15:51,52), and together caught up to meet the Lord.

VI. **That We Shall Be Forever with the Lord (v. 17).**
    Jesus' prayer answered (John 17:24).
    The saints' desire granted (Ps. 17:15).
    That will be heaven.

VII. **That This Will Be an Awful Day for the Unbelieving.**
    "Sudden destruction" (1 Thess. 5:3).
    "Everlasting destruction" (2 Thess. 2:9).

VIII. **That the Christian Should Be Looking for His Coming.**
    Not sleep as do others (1 Thess. 5:6).
    Now high time to awake (Rom. 13:11).

FREDERICK RADER

THE SECOND COMING OF CHRIST

Hebrews 9:28

Introduction

In God's plan for the salvation of men, Jesus was to come to the earth twice. The first time He came to give His life and shed His blood that we might be saved. The second time He will come in power and glory, "without a sin offering for salvation." We must accept the full benefits of His first coming to be prepared for His second coming, for the joy of His second coming is reserved for those "that look for Him," and only those who are prepared are looking for Him in genuine anticipation.

I. Christ's Second Coming Is to Be Personal (Acts 1:10,11).

His second coming is not to be identified with the coming of the Holy Spirit at Pentecost, with death, with the preaching of the Gospel among the nations or with any other invisible occurrence in the history of men; for His coming is "in like manner" as He went away. That is, it is to be personal and visible to His disciples.

II. The Time of Christ's Second Coming Is at the End of This Age (Matt. 24:14).

From the beginning of the Christian era the second coming of Christ has been imminent, and its approach has greater meaning for us than for any who have lived before us. By imminent we do not mean that Christ will come at some certain time, but rather that He may come at any time. We may not know the exact time of His coming; this knowledge is in the mind of God. But the Scriptures give certain signs that are to indicate that His coming draws nigh. These signs are:
   A. Lukewarmness in the church (Matt. 24:12; 2 Tim. 3:1-5).
   B. Distress and uncertainty among the nations (Matt. 24:7).
   C. Want of equity in the economic sphere (James 5:1-8).
   D. The general deterioration of the home (2 Tim. 3:2).

III. The Master and Purpose of His Coming (1 Thess. 4:13-17).
   A. The Lord shall descend with a shout. The coming will be sudden, personal and glorious.
   B. The dead in Christ shall be resurrected, and the living in Christ shall be translated.

C. The saved of the ages, constituting the Church, the Bride, the Lamb's wife, will go on to the marriage supper of the Lamb (Rev. 19:7-9).

D. The Great Tribulation shall then come to the earth (Rev. 16-19).

IV. Preparation for His Coming (Matt. 24:44).

To the Master's word, "Surely, I come quickly," does your heart respond, "Amen. Even so, come Lord Jesus"?

J. B. CHAPMAN

HE IS COMING AGAIN

John 14:3

I. The Son of God Came Once.

A. When we commemorate that first advent, we do so as that of One who came to save.

B. At the Lord's Table we bring to mind the advent of the Son of God into our life.

C. Let us come to the Table to clasp the hands of our Redeemer, and to receive Him so that we may be made "more than conquerors."

D. We come not only to receive, but also "to show forth the Lord's death till He come" (1 Cor. 11:26).

II. He Who Came Once Will Come Again.

A. Early disciples anticipated an early fulfillment of the promise, and were scoffed at for so doing. "Where is the promise of His coming?" (2 Peter 3:4).

B. Christ did not return while they lived. The promise is not yet fulfilled.

C. The Son of God will come the second time as Judge.

D. We ought to expect this second advent (Titus 2:1-3). So shall we be ready.

CONDENSED FROM JAMES DINWOODIE

WHY IS CHRIST COMING?

"Where is He that is born King of the Jews?" (Matt. 2:2).

He Is Coming:

1. To complete the Salvation of the Saints.

   "For our conversation (citizenship) is in heaven; from whence we look for the Savior, the Lord Jesus Christ: who shall change our vile body (the body of our humiliation), that it may be fashioned like unto His glorious body, according to the working whereby He is able even to subdue all things unto Himself" (Phil. 3:20; Rom. 8:22,23; Heb. 9:28; 1 Peter 1:5).

2. To be Glorified in His Saints.
   "He shall come to be glorified in His saints" (2 Thess. 1:10).

3. To be Admired in Those Who That Believe.
   "When He shall come to be glorified in His saints, and to be admired in all them that believe" (2 Thess. 1:10).

4. To Bring to Light the Hidden Things of Darkness.
   "Therefore judge nothing before the time, until the Lord come, who both will bring to light the hidden things of darkness, and will make manifest the counsels of the hearts" (1 Cor. 4:5).

5. To Judge All Men.
   "For the Father judgeth no man, but hath committed all judgment unto the Son" (John 5:22; 2 Tim. 4:1; Jude 14,15; Rev. 20:11-13).

6. To Destroy Death.
   "For He must reign, till He hath put all enemies under His feet. The last enemy that shall be destroyed is death" (1 Cor. 15:25,26).

7. To Reign as King.
   "The kingdoms of this world are become the kingdoms of our Lord, and of His Christ; and He shall reign forever and ever" (Rev. 11:15; Isa. 24:23; Dan. 7:14).

                                                              SELECTED

THE DAY OF THE LORD AS
A THIEF IN THE NIGHT

1 Thessalonians 5:2

If Scripture did not warrant this figure, in which the second coming of the Lord is compared to the act of a felon breaking into a house at night to plunder, we should not have suggested it. The comparison is suggested by our Lord Himself, "Watch therefore, for ye know not what hour your Lord doth come. If the good man of the house had known in what hour the thief would come, he would have watched."

I. The Day of the Lord.

By this expression must be meant a day in some unique sense His day; for all days are, in reality, days of the Lord of time.

A. By "the day of the Lord" is meant that day on which He will take the first place in the thoughts of His creatures.

B. It is the day on which He will bring the vast moral account between Himself and His responsible creatures to a close.

II. As a Thief in the Night.

What are the ideas suggested by this comparison?

A. It is suggestive of fear. The old prophets spoke of the coming day of universal doom as "the great and terrible day of the Lord," and we cannot but echo their language. It is during the years of time that men decide how they will meet the judgment.

B. It is suggestive of suddenness. There is the contrast which it will present to many of God's judgments in this present life. They approach with measured steps. Neither war nor famine nor pestilence come, generally, like a thief in the night. Are we looking for this sudden advent? A Christian's first practical anxiety should be expressed in His Master's words, "Lest coming suddenly He find me sleeping."

C. It is suggestive of that which cannot be prevented by our own efforts. We cannot prevent the coming of Christ in the clouds of heaven. We can prepare to meet Him, by judging ourselves in self-examination. We may erect each one in his own a tribunal, and bid our acts, words, our lives, all our life pass before it; and then we may hear, if we will, the echoes of the voice of Christ, in mercy, or in condemnation, as that voice will sound to us hereafter from the judgment throne. We may prepare for that day by setting apart some fixed time for making a business-like preparation for death. Death, like judgment, comes as a thief. Death is the antechamber of the judgment hall of Christ. To prepare for death is a man's most serious business during his life. "Ye are not in darkness that that day should overtake you as a thief." God grant it may be so with us.

H. P. LIDDON

"HE COMETH"

Psalm 96:13

1. The Believer's Expectation—He that shall come will come, and will not tarry (Col. 3:4; 1 John 3:2; Heb. 10:37).

2. The Believer's Attitude—Looking for that blessed hope; waiting for the Son from heaven (1 Thess. 1:10; Titus 2:13).

3. The Believer's Stimulus—Seeing that all these things shall be dissolved, what manner of persons ought ye to be? (2 Peter 3:11).

4. The Sinner's Dread—He cometh to judge the earth (Ps. 98:9).

5. God shall bring every work into judgment, with every secret thing, whether it be good or whether it be evil (Eccl. 12:14).

6. Behold. He cometh with clouds; and every eye shall see Him, and they also which pierced Him; and all kindreds of the earth shall wail because of Him (Rev. 1:7).

SELECTED

THE SECOND ADVENT

"Behold He cometh with clouds; and every eye shall see Him; and they also which pierced Him: and all kindreds of the earth shall wail because of Him" (Rev. 1:7).

God has appointed a day when He will judge the world in righteousness, by that man whom He has ordained—Jesus Christ. As certainly as the Son of God was raised from the dead, shall He come the second time without a sin-offering unto salvation. Brethren, we shall all appear before Him; all the generations that have preceded us; all our contemporaries; and all the generations that are unborn, shall be there. "Behold, He cometh with clouds," etc.

Our subject leads us to consider, I. The Judge, II. The Manner of His Coming, III. The Witnesses of His Appearing and IV. The Effects of His Decisions.

I. The Judge.

John has manifest reference to the divine Savior: "We shall stand before the judgment-seat of Christ." Here, then, it may be useful to consider some qualifications of the Son of man for the high office which He sustains.

A. As a judge of glorious dignity, of high, indisputable authority. Such, indeed, is His dignity, that He is the "brightness of His Father's glory, and the express image of His person; upholding all things by the word of His power." He is "King of kings, and Lord of lords; Heir of all things," etc. He is qualified for His high office.

B. By His perfection of omniscience. No man, however acute his discernment, can know the thoughts and intents of the heart. With Messiah is unbounded knowledge. "All things are naked," etc. "He searcheth the hearts," etc. "He needeth not that any should testify to man, for He knoweth what is in Him."

C. He is a Being of the most perfect equity. No quality more important in a judge than pure justice. Our divine Judge is perfectly free from all the partialities incident to humanity: "Judgment and justice are the habitations of His throne." "A scepter of righteousness is the scepter of His kingdom."

D. As a Judge He will be armed with almighty power. To express His omnipotence, He is styled in Scripture, "the only

Potentate, the King of kings," etc. "He doeth according to His will in the armies of heaven, and among the inhabitants of the earth." He is almighty. Power and strength belong to His perfections. When He was in the world, the wind and sea obeyed Him, and devils fled at His approach. Let us then consider,

II. The Manner of His Coming.

"In clouds." Jesus gave this reply when asked, "Art thou the Christ?" He answered: "I am: and ye shall see the Son of man sitting on the right hand of power, and coming in the clouds of heaven" (Mark 14:62; 13:26; Matt. 14:30; 26:64). The angels, at Christ's ascension, also declared that He should come again in like manner, as He had ascended, when a cloud received Him out of their sight (Acts 1:9-11). The apostle, also, describing the Lord's advent, says: "Then we, which are alive, shall be caught up together with them in the clouds, to meet the Lord in the air," etc. (1 Thess. 4:17). The Scriptures connect the visible appearance of our Lord with a magnificent train of angels, which is to constitute His retinue (Matt. 25:31). Notice,

III. The Witnesses of His Appearing.

"Every eye shall see Him." What a vast assembly! A nation—an empire—a quarter of the globe—whole of the present generation—all the generations past, and all that are yet unborn. In this assembly will be seen His friend and foes—Caiaphas and Annas, the high priests—the Scribes and Pharisees—the fickle multitude, who one day exclaimed, "Hosanna!" and the next, "Crucify Him! crucify Him!" There will be Pontius Pilate, who condemned, and Judas, who betrayed Him—Jews and Gentiles—barbarians and civilized—bond and free—great and small; yea, every eye shall see Him. Not one human being shall be excused, from Adam to the last-born of our race. Observe,

IV. The Consequences of His Coming.

"All nations shall wail because of Him." All nations have sinned against Him; multitudes of all nations have hated and rejected Him. To them the appearance of the Judge will be terrible indeed! He will then arraign them, try them, pronounce them guilty, and cause them to be thrust out, where there will be "weeping, wailing, and gnashing of teeth."

Application

1. It is a consolation that the Judge of all is the Savior of men. He once died for us; He now invites and entreats us to come to Him for pardon and life. "Kiss the Son, lest He be angry," etc. (Ps. 2:12). "Agree with thine adversary," etc. (Matt. 5:25).
2. We see the evil nature and dreadful consequences of sin. It is this that makes life wretched, death fearful, and judgment tremendous. Deliverance from it, therefore, is present happiness, and will lay a foundation for a blessed hope of meeting the descending Judge with joy, and not with grief.
3. To the incorrigibly wicked, that day of the Lord will be fearful indeed! (see Rev. 6:14-17; 2 Thess. 1:8).

DAVID SUTHERLAND

THE MARRIAGE SUPPER OF THE LAMB

I. The Lamb. Denotes:
   A. Gentleness. "Brought . . . the slaughter" (Isa. 53:7).
   B. Substitution. "In the stead of his son" (Gen. 22:13).

II. The Supper.
   A. The supper is free to all (Luke 14:21).
   B. It is the last meal of the day.

III. The Marriage.
   A. A time of unity. "They two shall be one (Eph. 5:31).
   B. It should be a time of joy.

IV. The Call.
   A. "Blessed are they which are called" (Rev. 19:9).

SELECTED

THE THREE R'S OF THE
LORD'S COMING AGAIN

Most of us are familiar with the Three R's specially connected with the: *First Coming*—to save from man's Run by Redemption through His blood and Regeneration of the Holy Spirit.

Here are three R's in connection with our Lord's coming again:

I. **The Reality.** Is it a "fable" or a Scriptural truth? Note that—

A. The Savior's own Declaration: "I will come again and receive you unto Myself" (John 14:1).

B. The Special Angelic Confirmation of the Savior's "I will" by "This same Jesus shall so come" (Acts 1:11).

C. The Special Apostolic Revelation: "Received" direct from glory. "The Lord Himself shall descend" (1 Thess. 4:13-18).

II. **The Rapidity.** Perhaps the most striking feature of the Coming is the undreamt-of brevity of the Rapture. This thought is enforced—

A. By the Threefold Injunction of the last leaf of God's last message: Behold; Behold; surely I come quickly (Rev. 22:7, 12, 20).

B. By the Definite Statement in the chapter of fundamentals: "We shall be changed in a moment" (1 Cor. 15:51). The devil offered Christ all the kingdoms "in a moment." God will give Him all the redeemed as quickly—"in a moment." O what a moment!

C. By the Familiar Simile: "In the twinkling of an eye." You give your eye a twinkle. How rapid! Your "vile body" shall with equal rapidity be made like His "own glorious body."

III. **The Result.** Naturally we think of ourselves first. But what shall be the result of the appearing to Himself?

A. In the fullest sense, "He shall see of the travail of His soul, and He shall be satisfied" (Isa. 53:11).

B. As to Ourselves: Guilty, hell-deserving sinners, whom He justified in time, shall be manifestly glorified in eternity (Rom. 1:30).

C. The Church, now rent and split and divided shall be united. The prayer of 1800 years ago, "That they all may be one" (John 17:21), shall be manifestly and eternally answered.

The Central Glory of it all: "I will come again and receive you unto Myself." "Amen. Even so, come, Lord Jesus!"

HY PICKERING

HE IS COMING WITH CLOUDS

"Behold, He cometh with clouds; and every eye shall see Him, and they also which pierced Him: and all kindreds of the earth shall wail because of Him. Even so, Amen" (Rev. 1:7).

I. Our Lord Jesus Comes.
    A. This fact is worthy of a note of admiration—"Behold!"
    B. It should be vividly realized till we cry, "Behold, He cometh!"
    C. It should be zealously proclaimed. We should use the herald's cry, "Behold!"
    D. It is to be unquestioningly asserted as true. Assuredly He cometh.

    It has been long foretold. Enoch (Jude 14).

    He has Himself warned us of it. "Behold, I come quickly!"

    He has made the sacred supper a token of it. "Till He come."
    E. It is to be viewed with immediate interest.

    "Behold!" for this is the grandest of all events.

    "He cometh," the event is at the door.

    "He," Who is your Lord and Bridegroom comes.
    F. It is to be attended with a peculiar sign—"with clouds."

    The clouds are the unique tokens of His Second Advent.

    The tokens of the divine presence. "The dust of His feet."

    The pillar of cloud was such in the wilderness.

    The emblems of His majesty.

    The ensigns of His power.

    The warnings of His judgment. Charged with darkness and tempest are these gathered clouds.

II. Our Lord's Coming Will Be Seen by All.
    A. It will be a literal appearance. Not merely every mind shall think of Him, but "Every eye shall see Him."
    B. It will be beheld by all sorts and kinds of living men.
    C. It will be seen by those long dead.
    D. It will be seen by His actual murderers, and others like them.
    E. It will be manifest to those who desire not to see the Lord.
    F. It will be a sight in which you will have a share.

III. His Coming Will Cause Sorrow. "All kindreds of the earth shall wail because of Him."

    A. The sorrow will be very general. "All kindreds of the earth."

    B. The sorrow will be very bitter. "Wail."

    C. The sorrow proves that men will not be universally converted.

    D. The sorrow also shows that men will not expect a great deliverance from Christ's coming.

    They will not look to escape from punishment.

    They will not look for Annihilation.

    They will not look for Restoration.

    If they did so, His coming would not cause them to wail.

    E. The sorrow will, in a measure, arise out of His glory, seeing they rejected and resisted Him. That glory will be against them.

- Even so, Lord Jesus, come quickly! In the meanwhile, it is not heaven that can keep Thee from me; it is not earth that can keep me from Thee; raise Thou up my soul to a life of faith with Thee: let me even enjoy Thy conversation, whilst I expect Thy return. —BISHOP HALL

- "Every eye shall see Him." Every eye; the eye of every living man, whoever he is. None will be able to prevent it. The voice of the trumpet, the brightness of the flame, shall direct all eyes to Him, shall fix all eyes upon Him. Be it ever so busy an eye, or ever so vain an eye, whatever employment, whatever amusement it had the moment before, will then no longer be able to employ it, or to amuse it. The eye will be lifted up to Christ, and will no more look down upon money, upon books, upon land, upon houses, upon gardens.
  Your eyes and mine. O awful thought! Blessed Jesus! May we not see Thee as through tears; may we not then tremble at the sight! —DR. DODDRIDGE

- "And the Lord turned and looked upon Peter. . . . And Peter went out and wept bitterly." So shall it be, but in a different sense, with sinners at the day of judgment. The eye of Jesus as their judge shall be fixed upon them, and the look shall awake their sleeping memories, and reveal their burdens of sin, and shame—countless and cursed crimes, denials worse than Peter's since life-long and unrepented of, scoffings at love that wooed them, and despisings of mercy that called them—all these shall pierce their hearts as they behold the look of Jesus.

And they shall go out and flee from the presence of the Lord—go out never to return, flee even into the outer darkness, if so be they may hide them from that terrible gaze. And they shall weep bitterly—weep as they never wept before, burning, scalding, tears, such as earth's sorrow never drew—weep never to be comforted, tears never to be wiped away. Their eyes shall be fountains of tears, not penitential and healing, but bitter and remorseful—tears of blood—tears that shall rip the heart in two, and deluge the soul in endless woe.   —ANONYMOUS

C. H. SPURGEON

THE JUDGMENTS

   I. The judgment of believers as sinners is on the cross of Christ (Rom. 6:6-8; Heb. 10:17; 1 John 4:7; John 3:18; 2 Cor. 5:14-21; 1 Peter 2:24).

  II. The judgment of saints (works)—at the "judgment seat of Christ" after the saints have been caught up (1 Thess. 4:14, 17; 1 Cor. 4:1-5; 3:13-15; 2 Cor. 5:9,10; Rom. 14:10, 12).

 III. The judgment of the "quick" ("living") nations (Acts 10:42; 2 Tim. 4:1; 1 Peter 4:5; 1 Cor. 6:2; Matt. 25:31-45; Acts 17:31). "Inhabited earth." (Day of Judgment, 1,000 years.)

  IV. The judgment of the "dead"—"Great White Throne" at the close of the Millennium (Matt. 10:15; 11:21,22; 12:41,42; Rev. 20:12, 15; 2 Peter 2:9; 3:7; Jude 6; Rom. 2:15,16).

   V. The judgment of angels (1 Cor. 6:2; Jude 6; 2 Peter 2:4; Rev. 20:10; Matt. 25:41).

T. C. ROUNDS

THE SECOND COMING UNEXPECTED

I. **Jesus Is Coming Again.**
Our God shall come (Ps. 1:3).
The Lord Himself shall descend from heaven (1 Thess. 4:16).
This same Jesus . . . shall so come (Acts 1:11).
The Son of Man shall come in the glory of His Father (Matt. 16:27).
They shall see the Son of Man coming in the clouds of heaven (Matt. 24:30).
Behold, He cometh with clouds; and every eye shall see Him (Rev. 1:7).
The voice of my Beloved! behold, He cometh (S. Sol. 2:8).

II. **And That Soon and Unexpectedly.**
Yet a little while, and He that shall come will come, and will not tarry (Heb. 10:37).
Behold, I come quickly; and My reward is with Me (Rev. 22:12).
Surely I come quickly (Rev. 22:20).
Ye know not what hour your Lord doth come (Matt. 24:42).
Ye know not when the Master of the house cometh, at even, or at midnight, or at the cock-crowing, or in the morning (Mark 13:35).

III. **To Receive His Own Children.**
He shall gather together His own elect (Matt. 24:31).
Ye shall be caught up . . . to meet the Lord in the air (1 Thess. 4:17).
Thou shalt receive me to glory (Ps. 73:24).
I will come again, and receive you unto Myself (John 14:3).

IV. **That They May Be with Him.**
There where I am, there ye may be also (John 14:3).
Where I am, there shall also My servant be (John 12:26).
Father, I will that they also, whom Thou hast given Me, be with Me where I am (John 17:24).
Thou shalt be with Me in Paradise (Luke 23:43).
With Christ, which is far better (Phil. 1:23).

V. In a Place Prepared for Them.

Come, ye blessed of My Father, inherit the kingdom prepared
for you (Matt. 25:34).

Eye hath not see . . . the things which God hath prepared for
them that love Him (1 Cor. 2:9).

Men have not heard. . . . O God, beside Thee, what He hath
prepared for him that waiteth for Him (Isa. 64:4).

An inheritance incorruptible, and undefiled reserved in
heaven for you (1 Peter 1:4).

I go to prepare a place for you (John 14:2).

FOOTSTEPS OF TRUTH

THE PROMISE OF THE LORD'S COMING

The New Testament is full of promises that He will return: Acts
1:9-11; Revelation 3:3-11; John 14:2,3; Revelation 16:15; 22:7, 12,
20; Hebrews 9:28; Acts 3:19-21.

He is coming back:

I. To raise the righteous dead: Isaiah 26:19; John 11:25;
Daniel 12:13; John 5:28,29; Philippians 3:10,11; 1 Thessalonians
4:13-16; 1 Corinthians 15:20, 23, 52; Revelation 20:4-6.

He is also coming back:

II. To change the living (as Enoch, Gen. 5:24, and Elijah, 2
Kings 2:11): Isaiah 26:20-21; Luke 16:26,27, 34-37; 1 Thessalonians
4:15-17; Matthew 25:6-10; Luke 21:36; 1 Thessalonians 5:4, 8-10;
Luke 12:35-38; 1 Corinthians 15:51; Revelation 3:10; Revelation
12:5.

SELECTED

THE OUTCOME OF WAITING FOR CHRIST

1. Unceasing **Watchfulness**.
   "Shall find watching" (Luke 12:37).
2. Unswerving **Fidelity**.
   "To every man his work" (Mark 13:34).
3. Unwearied **Patience**.
   "Be ye also patient" (James 5:8).
4. Unflinching **Obedience**.
   "Shall find so doing" (Matt. 24:46).
5. Increasing **Holiness**.
   "Unblameable in holiness" (1 Thess. 3:13).
6. Unfailing **Comfort**.
   "Comfort one another" (1 Thess. 4:18).
7. Unending **Work**.
   "Occupy, till I come" (Luke 19:13).

—SELECTED

THE JUDGMENT OF GOD

I. Judgment will be universal:
   A. God has prepared throne to judge the world (Ps. 9:7,8).
   B. Goad has appointed a day to judge the world (Acts 17:31).
   C. God is judge of all (Heb. 12:23).
   D. Appointed to die; then the judgment (Heb. 9:27).
   E. This includes the saints (Rom. 14:9, 12).
   F. It also includes the wicked (Rev. 20:11-15).

II. Judgment will be righteous:
   A. Shall not judge of world do right? (Gen. 18:25).
   B. Righteousness and judgment, the habitation of throne (Ps. 89:14; 97:2).
   C. Judgment, according to truth (Rom. 2:1-5).
   D. Judgment, not after sight and hearing (Isa. 11:3).
   E. God tries the reins of the heart (Jer. 11:20).
   F. Judgment, according to will of God (John 5:30).
   G. Angels cry: "Righteous are judgments" (Rev. 16:5-7).
   H. Much people cry: "Righteous are judgments" (Rev. 19:13).
   I. "How unsearchable are His judgments" (Rom. 11:33).

H. W. FROST